7 Occult Money Rituals

The Keys to Authentic Financial Magick

Henry Archer

Pb

paratine
books

Copyright © 2017 by Henry Archer
Illustrations © 2017 by Zachary Davidson

All rights reserved.

Published worldwide by Paratine Books, London, England.

The publisher, author and illustrator have provided this book for personal use only. You are not permitted to make the book publicly available in any way. Infringement of copyright is against the law.

The illustrations in this book are reproductions of hand-drawn images from the author's collection, and are subject to copyright.

The author and the publisher assume no responsibility for your actions should you choose to use the ideas presented in this book.

7 Occult Money Rituals

The Secrets of Money Magick	7
The Powers of Financial Magick	9
The Experience of Money	13
How Money Magick Works	15
The Secrets of Occult Finance	19
Learn from Yourself	25
How to Perform Rituals	29
Ritual One: The Rejection of Personal Poverty	31
Ritual Two: Opening to Financial Growth	37
Ritual Three: Break Through Financial Barriers	43
Ritual Four: A Petition for Riches	49
Ritual Five: Attract a Sum of Money	55
Ritual Six: Increase Wages or Income	59
Ritual Seven: Improve Financial Luck	63
Make Some Money	65
Revelations of Knowledge	66

The Secrets of Money Magick

Receiving money is pleasant. Having and enjoying money is a warming experience. When you get money through magick, it's one of the best feelings in the world. But is it really possible?

When all else fails, magick offers real hope. But if you've got even half a brain, you're probably filled with doubt. If you're new to this thing called magick, it sounds too good to be true, or perhaps even frightening. If you're an experienced occultist, you're wondering about my credentials, and whether I'm just here to make a quick buck out of gullible readers. All fair. But consider this:

The very worst money magick in the world should make you at least $5, right? So, you're safe. You'll get your money back. You want more than a few dollars? Good. That desire will get you somewhere.

There are seven rituals here. If you use them, you're going to be able to cover the cost of this book, even if this is the worst magick in the world, because even weak magick is going to make you a few dollars. And trust me; this is not the worst magick in the world.

I'm promising you five dollars? No, I'm promising you a life where magick can bring you more and more and more, with money increasing forever. But that's a big claim, so forget about it for now, start small, and let this money magick work and build and grow and reward you.

All I ask of you is that you read with an open mind. If you're new to magick, you already believe it's *possible* or you'd never have bought this book. Be open to that feeling. If you already know magick inside out, be open to the idea that I might have something new for you. That's all.

I said back there that weak magick will make you $5, but I believe this is great magick, and I say that not through pride, but out of respect to the wise and knowledgeable mentors and guides that I have learned from. Although my personal creativity went into these rituals, it is based on the work of those who taught me. Work this magick well and you can make a lot of money. You can make life easier. And I say this to take the pressure off you.

When you hand over your money for a book, it can feel tense, worrying, like you've been deceived. You get buyer's remorse and worry the magick's just a joke. It's not a joke, and if you give it a go – there's *nothing* more important than giving it a go - it will work.

This book contains rituals of alchemy that change your very reality. You'll discover the six secret names of the archangel Metatron to access wealth. I reveal the four gnostic angels that break through financial barriers and show you a secret pathworking technique that accesses the power of ancient gods. I believe you will be thrilled by what you discover. Which leads to one big question.

If I know the occult secrets of money-making, why would I share them with you? Shouldn't I be sipping cocktails overlooking my infinity pool instead of wasting my time writing a book like this? It's one of the best questions you could ever ask, and when I answer it, you'll get a much better understanding of money magick, and exactly how it works.

Some of what follows might sound like pointless theory that you don't need. All you want is magick! I understand, but I can assure you that what comes first in this book is not just a bundle of thoughts and ideas; it's not just me being a loudmouth about my magick; and it's not a distraction. What you find in these opening pages is the very gateway into the magick.

I'll answer that question, about why I'm sharing my magick by letting you in on two big secrets in just a moment. But first, let me tell you how this magick's going to work for you.

The Powers of Financial Magick

I'm going to explain exactly what's coming up in the rest of the book.

The first ritual is about the rejection of personal poverty. You don't need to know anything about this magick, or believe anything, for it to work. You only need to do the magick. If you're in the depths of poverty, you begin to move away from those depths. If you're already doing OK with money, the ritual removes the fear that poverty can ever return.

The second ritual will remove your financial desperation. When you perform magick and feel an instant rush of *Where's my money?* then most often, the magick fails. This second ritual is a unique approach that helps you let go of urgent need. When you release your need (no matter how huge your actual needs may be – debts, bills, all that trouble) you will find a space in which you can accept and receive a new financial future.

The third ritual removes the blockages that prevent wealth from coming to you. You might be burdened by a fear of money, guilt about money, or other deep emotions that make you poor, or less rich than you want to be. This ritual eases the blockages away.

The fourth ritual is a petition for riches, and this is a master working that helps to attract money into your life over the coming year. It makes every opportunity a stronger opportunity, and makes it easier for financial luck to swing your way.

The first four rituals should be performed by everybody who reads this book. The remaining three rituals are optional, and can be used as required.

The fifth working is designed to attract a specific sum of money, to solve a problem or fulfil a desire.

The sixth working increases your wages, or income from business or sales.

The seventh ritual increases your luck in games of chance, including lotteries, card games and any form of gambling. This is not the best way to get rich, but if you like gambling, you'll get better results.

I know you're probably tempted to skip the first four rituals and get to the good ones, but if you look carefully, you'll see the first four *are* the good ones. These are the foundations that make the rest of the magick work. This will take you a few weeks. Yes, weeks. I know there's a trend of creating magick books where it takes just seconds to do the magick and you get results. I love that magick too, but *only when it works*. I'm not going to deceive you into thinking you can get money flowing in minutes. Get ready for a few weeks of magickal effort. It's easier than losing weight. Easier than going to the gym. Easier than working harder for money.

If you're itching to know what sort of magick this is, you're probably trying to guess whether it's ceremonial magick, or something to do with kabbalah, or sigils, or witchcraft and spellworking. The magick comes from many traditions and has been made into something new. Some occultists would label this as Chaos Magick because anything that doesn't fit in with their dogmatic rituals must be labelled as Chaos Magick. There's no shame in Chaos Magick – it's a way of using rituals and technologies from many traditions to get results. But in 'pure' Chaos Magick you *pretend* to believe, rather than actually believing in the entities you call on. I do believe. It doesn't matter whether *you* believe in the reality of the entities, or whether you think the gravity waves of your mind are shaping the flow of reality. But I believe that the spirits called in these rituals are real, and I have great respect for the powers. That is how the magick will be presented to you. What I don't believe is that you have to do ten hours of ceremonial preparation to get a good result.

For some people who use this magick, everything aligns, and very quickly, money turns up. It *can* happen within minutes. But it might take weeks. You've bought the book, so have a think, what would you rather achieve? Money? Or no money? If you want money, let it take a while to come to you, if it takes a while.

Desperation is for losers.

Patience is for the prosperous.

And when you read, don't jump ahead. What comes up in the following chapters is almost more important than the spells and rituals. If it sounds like I'm grousing about irrelevant ideas, take another look. The secrets in the upcoming chapters aren't coarse opinions or philosophies, but the energy that lies beneath the magick.

If you take all this in, the magick will work, and the more you use it, the more it works. The more you believe and live a life of magick, the more you have a magickal life.

The Experience of Money

You are in a unique position. I can't guess how rich or poor you might already be. I doubt you're homeless or earning less than minimum wage. I also doubt that you're earning more than $100,000 a year. I could be wrong, but I have found that a desire for magickal knowledge is driven by need, and those will too little often can't imagine that magick works, and those with a relatively high income are trapped in conventional thinking. There are, of course, many exceptions. But it's important to know that you are trying to improve your *personal* finances.

If you target your magick to bring more money, it can make you rich, but it's not probable that will happen overnight. What magick will do is lift you from your current financial plane. You are stuck in a plane of existence where you are earning an amount that feels comfortable and *believable* to you. Magick will take you, step by step and stage by stage, to new levels of income.

If you are earning very little, the changes will likely be small but significant, at first. They should always be appreciated. If magick brings you a dollar and you do nothing but sneer, the potency of magickal flow is tightened by the grip of your cynicism. Find some enthusiasm for supernatural income, even if that new income is not immediately or obviously useful to you. This is true even if you're already earning a large income. If you're earning $100,000, then a $100 magickal result isn't going to make you thrilled. But *let* yourself be thrilled.

When you cause change, through magickal acts, you need to appreciate and acknowledge what you have achieved. This is how you grow, how your belief shifts and how in time, your income changes to a plane of reality that once seemed unbelievable to you.

It is very difficult to know what level of income you truthfully desire. Those who earn the least are also, sadly, the least skilled at this. In fact, it is so difficult to know how wealthy you want to be that I say you should let go of the idea completely. You don't need to know where you're going. You only need to take steps in the right direction.

This magick helps you achieve your goals by removing the things that stop money coming to you, and then attracts money into your life. As this happens, you will grow and learn and become accustomed to money, and be able to earn more. This is not always a quick process, but it can be at times. All you need to do is read the instructions for each ritual and follow them.

How Money Magick Works

A few years ago, most practical magick books were, to put it candidly, pure trash. If you wanted to do practical magick you had to join an (expensive) magickal order, or buy lots of old, obscure and expensive books, or be very lucky, and then do a lot of work to even begin to guess what sort of ritual could possibly work. It was an abysmal situation for the would-be occultist. The internet made it all worse because it's filled with spells and rituals that may as well be made up by beginners or lunatics. But things have changed.

There are now lots of books, all giving out practical magick with methods you can use. This is good. The magick works. Not all of it works, and some of those books and weird magickal courses are nothing but fiction, but be thankful for the fact that you can *actually try magick*. If you want magick, it's there for the taking. It might take you a while to find magick that you resonate with, but if you sense there is magick there for you, I guarantee that there is.

A couple of decades ago, if you wanted to do magick, it would have been damned near impossible. You'd buy a book on occultism and find hundreds of pages of information about energy, and theories about the spheres of existence, and the most ego-driven opinions about reality, but almost *nothing* you could actually *do*. Occultism was all theory and opinions. Now you can get into workable magick on the day that you decide to. You can do magick today.

There are rituals you can do, processes you can try, and outcomes that you *might* get. You might not always get those outcomes, but let's be honest, you don't get everything you want first-time-every-time. Do you get a spectacular meal every time you go to a restaurant? No. You usually get your meal (although not always!), but what I'm being so painfully honest about here is that you need to go easy on the magick. We live in such an entitled age that people try magick, wait five minutes and then whine like babies if it doesn't work instantly. The magick owes you *nothing*. Let me be clear.

If it doesn't work, you're doing it wrong.

What can you do about this? Read the instructions and do the magick. Do more magick. Practice. Get better. It's really easy anyway, and doesn't take long, but it's like drawing or running or playing hockey – the more you do it, the better you get at it. And the more you do it, the less you'll panic and fume and worry and work yourself up about one result.

If this sounds harsh, get a refund on this book and carry on with your normal life. Magick works, and all magick needs is for you to line up with its methods, follow the instructions, do the work.

Don't be idiotic about it either. Ask for millions and you get nothing. Ask for just a bit more than seems possible and things happen. Money turns up. If at first you don't succeed, work at it. Magick will respond.

Does this make me sound like an arrogant ego-maniac, preaching about mastery of the occult? I can live with that because all this is said to help you. I'm not showing off, but I want to help you see the serious, undeniable truth.

Magick works if you work the magick properly.

Doing that is easy.

If those words make you think I'm an idiot, you're very welcome to your opinion. I'm being forceful, and you might even say harsh, but this all needs to be said.

If it seems too harsh, remember that we are on the same side. I want you to *like* magick, and I want it to *work* for you. What I say here is expressed without spectacle, to make life easier for you, by telling you the important truth now. I'm tired of occultists making excuses for their readers and students. If magick fails you, then you have failed magick, and you need to work with more focus, more energy, with better choices, better timing, a more open mind, or something else that's revealed in these pages. All the ideas are spread through this book, so read it again and again if you need to, and get it to work. It's as easy as that.

The position you're in now - that's not your fault. You may have spent more money than you have, planned badly, budgeted hopelessly and fumbled with your finances. But if you're poor, struggling or wanting more, an entire culture has been designed to keep you this way.

It's no fun being without money. You can tell yourself that it's meant to be, or that it's more spiritual, but I think that being poor is merely suffering. If you're suffering from lack, I know how that feels and I want it to change for you. It's not your fault that you feel this way, but it's up to you whether you get out of this situation.

The magick in this book comes from many sources, and has been shaped and clarified by practicing magicians over the past few decades, sometimes based on ideas that are a hundred years old, and often influenced by magick that is thousands of years old. This is Financial Magickal Technology.

If you know nothing about the occult, yet, this won't mean much to you. If you've been involved in the occult for years, you might shake your head in disbelief, as you have no interest in gnostic magick, or you might think Jovian magick needs to be much more ceremonial. This is where we are: either put your dogmatic beliefs and fears aside, or use the magick. It really is your choice.

There are rituals based on ancient magickal texts like *Sefer Raziel ha-Melakh*. Such ancient texts are written in Hebrew and are the source works that have inspired most of the magick in the Western tradition. By going back to the source, it's easier to create pure and powerful magick. But there's also magick that has nothing to do with this, coming from more obscure gnostic sources, such as the *Nag Hammadi Scriptures*, with angels that you've never heard of. Some of the magick might feel more like rustic spellcasting or pathworking. I don't care where it comes from or what it's called, if it works.

Whatever your religion, you can get this magick to work quickly and easily. Some of it will, I admit, seem too simple to be effective, but I'm not going to make it more complicated just to convince you. Do what's written and know that this magickal technology is complete, workable and a well-oiled machine that will work for you if you are willing to fire it into life.

Some of the ideas here are not widely known outside of organized occultism. Ten years ago, it would have been seen as occult heresy to share this sort of material. I think I'll be forgiven for sharing these ideas because they are meaningless unless you use them. The knowledge is harmless and only becomes powerful when you choose to become an occultist and actually perform a ritual. The ideas, methods and techniques are modest and they work, but just because they've been secret doesn't mean they have to stay secret.

The Secrets of Occult Finance

Ok, let's get back to that question. If I'm so loaded with cash, why do I waste my time selling a cheap little magick book? Firstly, cheap little magick books work, and that makes me feel good for you. I get pleasure out of that. But also, the astonishing truth is that when you share the secrets of magick, your power increases. My mentor told me this, and said that every time he taught me, *he* benefited more than I did. In teaching me, *he* learned, and in passing on magick, *he* became more powerful.

By sharing what I know with you, my own personal power will increase. Now if this tempts you to share the book with millions of people by pirating it and giving it away, let me tell you that's not the kind of sharing I mean. Piracy is a habit for the poor only – taking stuff for free only fills you with more feelings of being unable to afford. It's better to go without than to steal. This isn't a lecture on morals, but magickal truth. Occultists who steal make themselves poor. Those who steal magickal secrets make themselves truly sick with poverty. By purchasing the book legally, you take an important step to magickal wealth. If you steal it, every page curses you to remain poor.

Sharing *is* power. Every great occultist knows this, but it is rarely talked about. When you teach knowledge that is *unique to you*, your power increases. You only benefit when you share something original.

The magick in this book was developed by me, and although based on many centuries of knowledge, and the ideas and input of my mentor and other companions in magick, it has been made original and workable by me. I have shared it with many people, privately, during the past eleven years, and seen its astonishing power. I have faith in this magick and am proud to share it, and I know that sharing it will increase my power.

You could say, at this point, that I am nothing without you. Unless you learn this magick, and appreciate it and make it a part of your life, I have not shared my creation. This is why

I want it to work for you. I want you to know that you were right to buy this book, and that you are giving to me, just as I am giving to you.

You should understand that I have written this book for three reasons: I enjoy writing about this wonderful subject, it will make me some money, and it will increase the power of my magick because I am sharing my own personal occult practices.

By purchasing this book, *you* do three things; you make a sacrifice (only a few dollars, but still a sacrifice); you show some trust in magick (not a whole load of trust, but some, and that helps); and you commit time and energy to putting the principles to work (which is what it's all about). All these things give *you* power.

The small sacrifice you've made is hugely significant, and, thankfully, is the only sacrifice you need to make. Your trust, although shaky, is still trust. And your commitment to put time and energy into the magick is in itself an undertaking of magick. Your magick has already begun.

You might still be worried that I'm just taking your money for profit, and that's OK, but here's a really important step if you want to unlock money. Get over the idea that I've written this book to make a quick dollar. Why? Because it will harm your magick if you are filled with doubt and resentment and horror at somebody making a profit.

If you think like a poverty-ridden loser, you'll be as wealthy as one.

Is that really what you want?

Profit is good, and everybody who works or creates *should* make a profit. If you think otherwise, you're essentially calling for people to work as unpaid slaves. And yet you'd be amazed at how many people believe everything should be supplied free. If you believe that, if you hate money and earnings and profit so much, you will *never* earn as much as the rich.

Also, think about this: do you really want to take financial advice from somebody who doesn't make money? Come on! You don't learn about wealth from poor people. Look for successful authors and learn from them. Take your advice from those who already have money, not from those who are desperate for it.

So yes, I will make some money out of you, but *get over it*. That's only one of my motivations, and it doesn't harm you, so let it be. If you do the magick, you'll make a fortune for yourself eventually. And the real gift is that you learn to use magick. That's something you can use to improve your whole life.

Take a moment and imagine that this book sells really well, and I *do* make a lot of money from it. Does that make you resent me? If you find yourself resenting an author for charging you a measly, tiny fee for years of knowledge and work, then your entire financial world view is so screwed up you're going to find it hard to get money flowing freely. An attitude like that is destructive to your magick. I *should* make some money from this book, shouldn't I? You pay the local baker for a cake, don't you? Do you hate your baker for making a profit? You know what? I bet that baker isn't working for the love of it, or to spread a love of baking. That baker is doing it for the money. This does not make the baker evil. If you think it does, you've associated money with evil.

Let's get this clear; I'm never going to make a fortune from writing about the occult, because only a very small number of readers warm to this subject, but if I did make a fortune, you should be glad for me.

Notice how you felt when you read that. Did it make you really uncomfortable? If so, one of the most important rituals you can do is ritual three, to clear the emotional financial blockages that plague you, so that you can enjoy money.

If you're wise, you'll see that *none* of this is actually about me, my money and my book. Not a word of it. If you're clever, you'll see that I'm guiding you to one of the *most important principles* of financial magick; to thrive you need to settle into enjoying money, loving money, letting money come easily and feeling safe when it comes and goes, because you know it will always flow back.

Yes, it's OK to hate Wall Street, it's OK to resent the super-rich for their greed. It's OK to have politics that are about a more sharing and caring world. But be careful about letting your kind heart make you think of money as evil. If you do, money magick can make you a small profit, but not much more.

It's true that some of the rich are detestable. Money can be hoarded by the horrible, and earned by those who don't care how they fleece you or who they exploit, but you should not associate wealth and profit with evil. If you do, you remain poor. Know that making money, in ways that feel fair and beneficial to you, is a fine and truly spiritual way to live.

Have you read many magick books? Have you looked at the reviews, especially for the wealth, cash and financial books? The magick in those books works. I'm happy to say that about my competitors' books. A *lot* of magick works. I'm not going to boast about my magick and tell you to ignore everybody else and trust only me because I'm some super guru. It's *all* quite good. (Well, almost all. There are some weird, poor-looking authors who write books about being a billionaire with a few simple spells – but you won't fall for that will you?) But with the good books, even the best books, what you will notice is that even when the magick works for *most people*, you get these reviews where people say:

'Doesn't work. Waste of money.'

'Doesn't work. The author's just making money for himself.'

'Doesn't work, except to make more money for the rich author.'

Notice that pattern? It's not that the magick doesn't work – it works, you can see that because most people agree on that. But people who resent money, or hate money, or feel that everything should be free, or feel guilty about money – these are the people who will never get money magick to work. The reviews they write are completely true and honest, because for them, it *didn't* work and it *never* will. Not because it doesn't work. But because it *can't* work for people who resent money so deeply.

If you're struggling with this, I know how you feel, because I used to buy secret lottery tickets, hoping to get rich, but at the same time I would spit at the rich. I was so filled with bitterness about the wealthy – because I struggled to pay the bills and the rent and even to buy food – that I could never respect them. When you're struggling, it's hard. But you'll get there, and when you start using magick, it will all get easier.

Learn from Yourself

You don't need a magickal guru. I'll give you what you need to start performing financial magick, and then you only need your experience. But to get started, who am I to tell you what to do? What are my credentials? Do I have any right to talk about this magick?

I can tell you all sorts of stories about me and my magick, and who I've worked with and what I've achieved. Does it make a difference? Not one bit, because every word might be a lie. But here's' the big question: do *you* believe in magick?

What makes a difference is that you go ahead and try the magick and be open to it working. It's pretty easy.

Why am I going to such lengths to convince you that this isn't a con, that I'm not a charlatan and that magick is real? As a favor to you. This is not an attempt to convince you that I'm special and trustworthy. It's an opportunity for you to free up *your* mind. You are completely free to make up your own mind about me and this magick now. You can still think of this as a cheap trick if you decide to, but you are also free to see me in whatever light you want. And you are free to sense the possibility of magick. If you choose to trust me and the magick, there's a lot of enjoyment to be had, and a lot of money to be made by you.

Earlier, I promised you two big secrets, and there they are, in the chapters of the book you've just read: Sharing is power, and a respectful, fearless love of money brings more money. Like all the best secrets, these aren't secret at all. But they explain a lot about me, about you and about money.

The occult is not secret in the true sense of the word (which means hidden), because it's *not really hidden at all*. You can buy it on Amazon! It's hidden in plain sight like all the best secrets. Those who are enticed to explore magick, those who sense its power, they are the ones who benefit. If you are one of those people, magick absolutely will work for you.

But what's actually in the book? Am I going to have you

burning candles, reading Hebrew or calling to spirits?

If you've never done magick before, it can feel downright weird. You feel a bit ridiculous and wonder if what you're doing has any point, or whether you're making a fool of yourself. Do it anyway. Do it even if you're not sure about it. Get used to doing magick. I might tell you to do and say things that feel really unusual, but that's what you'd expect. It's magick. You don't need a cloak, or a magick circle. It's all pretty simple, and you'll get used to it.

If you've been working with magick for a few decades, you might wonder why I'm not sticking to the traditional rules. Well, because a lot of them aren't required. Chaos magick was a movement that changed magick forever because every open-minded occultist found that magick was a lot more workable than we ever knew. You could throw out hundreds of chants, days of preparation and even your wand. The magick here has been made simple. This is not new. Occultists have been doing this for nearly a hundred years, and they've been doing it with increasingly imaginative processes for the past forty years or so. Magick's now been purified down to the essentials. These essentials work.

Newcomers often worry about safety. The first moment you utter a magick word it can feel weird, as though you're opening the way for demons to take over your life. Or that accidents will happen to give you pay-outs. I can't really reassure you except to say that all the myths that are spread about karma and the spirits taking a payment from you – it's all disinformation, myth and cowardice.

Magick can feel weird, even spooky at times, but that's because its supernatural, not because it's dangerous. This book doesn't contain anything evil or demonic, but people will tell you that it does. For every great occult text, there's always a bunch of people claiming it includes demons. And there's a crazy reviewer on Amazon who reviews almost every occult book there is and says, 'Beware, this has secret demons and fallen angels.' There's nothing you can do except laugh. Or you can take these idiots seriously and panic about hidden demons.

Again, your choice.

Do what's written here and you are safe. If anything bad happens, it's either coincidence or you imagined it.

You might think you need to banish or put down a circle of protection. No. You don't. Not with this magick. In fact, I think that putting protection in place for magick that's as simple as this is a way of saying, 'I really want to fight magick off and keep things as normal as possible.' That's the opposite of what you want. The required names and words of protection are built into every ritual. That's what you need.

And forget about karma, the slingshot effect, the law of threefold return or any of that propaganda. I'm not the first to say this – but the universe does not balance everything out. The universe is filled with inequality. Magick gives you an advantage, but if you believe you somehow have to pay for that because the universe is all about fairness and balance, you're living in a different universe to me. You really need to watch the news and see that the universe is not about balance at all. It's about power.

You can increase your power by using magick – and then it's my hope you'll use that to do good, for yourself, for others and for the benefit of all. But that is actually your choice, and magick never makes you pay for what you've gained. Magick does not break your legs so that you get a big insurance pay-out. Magick does not smother your grandpa so you inherit his mansion. These are myths spread by people who hate magick. If any of that stuff was true, *nobody* would use magick.

I could write more, but the scared will always be scared, and the magickal will do magick. Do what you will.

For somebody who wants you to learn practical magick, I've talked a lot about the ideas behind the magick. This is important. Can you imagine trying to win a race if you didn't know the idea was to get across the line first? If you saw everybody running, you might join in, but you'd never know that you were meant to reach the ribbon before everybody else. With magick, and especially the technology of financial magick, there are some ideas you need to know. The good news is you've read them all now. If you ever struggle with this magick, I guarantee the answer will be found in the words you have just read. Go back to them if you need to. Otherwise, get ready to do money magick.

How to Perform Rituals

If you jumped ahead to this chapter, go back and read the first part of the book. It's not just the ideas and opinions of a loudmouth. It might seem like that, but I promise you there's gold in there. The first part of the book is a way of getting to the real energy that powers up this magick.

How do you think people go from rags to riches? It might be talent. It might be luck. It might be magick. You can hope your talent gets recognized, and you can wish for some luck, or you can use magick to make it happen the way you want. But you need to understand everything I've said up until now, and you need to be patient, persistent and you need to do the magickal work.

The change that occurs within you is as important as anything else. The first four rituals should be done in order, one after the other, taking your time and pausing if you want between rituals, or powering straight through. These rituals work on changing you and your relationship to money, and they work on shifting fortune in your favor. Used well, and with focus, they will transform your reality.

When the first four are complete, you can use the final three rituals. If you skip the first four, and try the final three, you *might* get results, but you'll be weakening your chances of success.

Do I have to keep mentioning patience? When you need money to pay bills, I know how hard it is. When you want money for something desperately, I get how patience is the last thing you want. But I promise that if you learn patience, you feed the rituals with trust, and that is the ambrosia of magick.

Ritual One: The Rejection of Personal Poverty

This ritual alone *can* make money flow to you from unexpected places. Might be a dollar here and there. Might be something totally unexpected. Might be nothing yet. Let it be whatever it will be, and remember that right now you're cultivating a powerful patience, and hooking up to Financial Magickal Technology.

The fact that you're going to do this ritual for quite a few days, without actually expecting money to turn up, is such a powerful move. It's a strategy that shocks your reality. Here you are, ready to do money magick, and you perform a ritual that might not even make money turn up. This act of magickal trust, of getting into the flow of magick, is one of the most powerful things you can do. But I'll stop going on about it and let you do the magick.

The ritual comes in two parts. One is empowerment and the other is diffusion – you charge the ritual, and then you let its energy spread out into your reality. You can start this ritual on any day of any month, without any concern about astrological timing. If you *want* to time the ritual according to astrological dates, you can begin the diffusion part of the ritual on a Thursday evening, on or shortly after a new moon. I would only do this if it was convenient, as I think the astrological influences are forces that can assist, rather than barriers to magick. If you have no interest in astrology, do the ritual whenever you want. It hardly makes any difference at all.

For the empowerment phase of the ritual you'll need a candle, any size, any color, but don't get one that's too huge or the ritual will take weeks rather than days.

A candle is a lump of grease with a piece of string through the middle. That's all. Only through an act of magick do you make it magickal, so any candle will do. Green, blue, black, whatever you want. I use ordinary white candles. That's what I suggest you do, but use whatever you like.

Some people get all uptight about candle colors and how

31

they correspond to certain planets or energies. If you're heavily into those correspondences, go ahead and use them (green and blue are popular for money), but don't let this sort of thing restrict you, and if you've never even heard of these correspondences, lucky you, you can ignore them.

This ritual is about rejecting your personal poverty. If you consider yourself wealthy already why are you reading this book? I assume that on some level you feel poverty, or fear it. Even if you're doing OK, making a good living, there is a sense of lack, of money missing from your life. This is what I mean by personal poverty. You may actually be so poor that you're taking regular trips to the food bank, or you may run your own company and want to break through to the next level of success. In magickal terms, whatever you lack is poverty. You can whither that poverty away through the symbolism of the candle.

But here's the trick. You don't actually push the poverty away, but expand the energy of wealth. Think of it like this. If I want to dry my clothes, I don't wring them out by hand and put in all that effort to make them dry. That leaves the clothes damp, hurts my hands and doesn't even get all the water out. What I do is hang the clothes in the sunshine, and they become dry without effort. The sun and the wind does the work. In this ritual, you create feelings that are the sun and the wind of the magick. By building up the feeling of easy wealth, you purge the damp misery of poverty.

The first step is to empower the candle, to make it a ritualistic object. You fill the candle with feelings of wealth, with the reality of wealth, and then as it burns and turns to heat, light and nothingness, that wealth spreads out into your world, into your natural self and your way of living.

Instead of trying to have positive thoughts, or trying to shut out negative thoughts, you create a powerful magickal object that is filled with the sensation of wealth, and then you transform it from the real and physical to the invisible. Burning the candle is a way of making your magickal object disappear from the real world and appear in the astral plane. The thoughts and feelings that have blessed your candle are transformed into the alchemical ether.

Do not light the candle, but lay it on its side on any surface where you want to work. Right now, it's not a magickal object. It becomes one when you choose to make it magickal. Your goal is to put feelings of wealth and receiving into the candle. There are many versions of this process throughout occultism, and most involve intense force and wilful imagination, but this is quite difficult. To make it easier, I suggest using mere fantasy. We love to fantasize, and we love imagining having more money. That's why you bought this book, and that's why this process is easy even if you think your imagination isn't good enough. If you have the desire for more money, you can fantasize about having more. We do this with a magickal slant, to make it resonate on a deeper level of reality, but it's as easy as daydreaming.

In the fantasy, all you do is imagine what it would feel like to have more money than you want or need. At this moment, you may have desires and needs, and many things that you want, and dreams of great wealth. But something you may never have experienced is that moment when you realize that nothing seems to cost anything anymore, when there are no restrictions on what you can have. This is a very real feeling that comes with wealth. It is, of course, not entirely accurate. I could not afford to buy a skyscraper or a small country, but it doesn't matter, because I have no interest in doing so. But as you become wealthy, you notice that the bills get paid without effort, and then you find that buying new clothes –which once seemed so taxing on your finances – barely affects you. You buy a car with cash rather than credit. You do the same with a house. You always have money to spare. This life is not going to come to you tomorrow, but I can tell you that this feeling is what you're really looking for. Ease.

The ease of money, the ease of knowing there will always be enough. You can book that trip without even checking your bank balance. You can do anything that takes your fancy and you won't even feel the strain. If you are poor or struggling, you may want to imagine problems solved, but trust me that you will solve your problems if you focus now on imagining the ease you will feel when you have more than you want more need.

To get into this it might help to imagine paying off all your bills, and imagine the trips, the houses, the cars and the fun things you can do with money, but for this ritual I ask that you focus on the *feeling of ease* more than anything else. Imagine a life where you spend $300 at a restaurant and it feels great. Imagine paying hundreds of thousands of dollars in taxes and feeling good about it because you still have more than you could ever spend. Imagine the absolute ease of buying anything you desire. How you do this will be down to you because your fantasy is not the same as mine. The important thing is not to get carried away with lifestyle fantasies. Don't waste your time picturing a life with celebrities, or being rich enough to go to exclusive parties. That's focussing on a different feeling that's about glamour and glitz. That life might happen too, but what you're looking for right now is the feeling of *ease*. Why? Because when you actually get money, when you become wealthy (compared to where you are now), ease is the most surprising, powerful and lovely feeling you experience. It is real, it happens, and if you feel it now and put that feeling into your simple candle, that feeling can be scorched and burned into the future that's coming to you.

You can imagine situations of ease, like buying a car with a bank transfer rather than with a loan, or choosing the perfect house and knowing you won't even need a mortgage. You can probably come up with better examples that really stir your personal emotions.

You don't need to spend hours building up this feeling. It's all about the quality of the feeling, not the amount of time you put in. If, after thirty seconds, you can imagine the glorious ease of being so wealthy, then you're ready for the next step. If you have to coax yourself there, by fantasising a few different scenarios until you really begin to feel the ease, take your time. When you get the feeling, the next step is to transfer that feeling to the candle.

In magick, we use light. Light is a particle and a wave, which means it is physical and non-physical. It's the perfect symbol. It exists in the world and can be imagined within, and this gives imagined light great power. As you feel the ease of wealth, imagine a golden-white light within your body. It may be in your heart, your solar plexus, your belly, or this whole area, but it will almost certainly be felt in your torso, not your head. Let the light build up with the feeling of ease, and then let the light pour out of you and into the candle. The light carries the feeling of ease into the candle.

You are just pretending, on some level. You build up a feeling and pretend that the feeling is light, and then you pretend the light goes into the candle. It sounds a bit silly, but all magick sounds silly when you take a step back from it. So does ballroom dancing. So does a rock concert. So does watching movies. If you want it to work, do the work.

Your emotions do not need to be pure, your imagination does not need to be perfect, you do not need to believe that this is even real, but act as though this is worthwhile, act as though your feelings are being embedded in the molecules of the candle.

You may find that you only need to do this once. If it feels strong and ready, as though your feelings have sunk into the material of the candle, you are ready to move to the next stage (where you actually light it). If you have trouble generating the feeling of ease and projecting it as light, maybe take a week or so, once a day. Or do this part of the ritual ten times in one day. You can tell that what I'm saying here is that once you feel ready, you will know. But give yourself some credit and know that if you've followed the instructions, you've probably done a brilliant job. You don't need to work away at this for weeks.

Now all you do is burn the candle. At least once a day, light the candle, and be in the presence of its flame. You think nothing of it, don't even wonder about what's happening. All the build-up has worked the magick into this moment. In burning the candle, it is impossible for your subconscious to forget what's going on here. On a magickal level, you know that your thoughts are being transformed to light and heat, moving from the physical to the invisible and immaterial. You could stare at that candle and focus on these thoughts, but you'd be wasting your time. It works better when you ignore it.

Light the candle and do something else while the candle remains nearby. You should never leave a candle unattended, for obvious reasons. You might want to read a book, watch TV, cook dinner or do whatever else you do with your time. If you're going to leave the room, snuff out the candle and light it again another time.

Eventually, the candle will burn out. You'll be left with a very small amount of wax and wick. This in itself is symbolic of the fact that our efforts and thoughts and magickal workings are never entirely perfect, but that we put doubts aside, cast them away. So, discard this wax and wick. Throw it in the trash and let it be nothing to you.

The burning down of the candle might take just one afternoon if you've used a small candle and sit with it all afternoon. If you have a large candle and light it once a day for just a few minutes, it may take many months. Use whatever approach you like, but don't begin the next ritual until at least one full day has passed since the first lighting of the candle. You may prefer to wait until the entire candle ritual is over before proceeding to the next ritual, and if you have the patience, that's what I recommend.

Ritual Two: Opening to Financial Growth

The second ritual will remove or lessen your financial desperation, which opens you up to financial growth. You will let go of the urgent need.

This might sound like the opposite of what you want, but don't worry; this does not mean your real needs will vanish, and you won't lose your motivation. All you lose is damaging desperation, which clogs the mechanisms of magick. When desperation is removed, money flows. You will have bills to pay and financial needs, but this ritual will put you in the same mindset as the rich. You do not find rich people suffering from the intense pain of financial desperation. It is not a part of their reality and it should not be a part of yours. As the desperation is relieved, so you open up a space in your reality for a new level of financial success.

If you do this all by yourself it's a lot of effort, and it takes willpower and imagination. To make it easier, you work with angelic names which act as power words. That puts energy into the work for you.

Angels are most effective in magick when they are asked to make a change in your feelings. You're not asking for great riches. You're just asking for the angel to change how you feel, and angels are very obliging when it comes to this.

This ritual contains a sequence of names for the angel Metatron. These angelic names are taken from an ancient collection of manuscripts known as *Merkavah Rabbah*. If you want to do your own academic research look at MS. Oxf. 1531, but there is no need to do any research as the names are provided here with their correct pronunciation.

The angels you call on are Margioawiel, Tahnahriel, Gahpahiel, Ahaweziel, Sahsahngariah, Palisahiqiawn and Sahngahdiah.

It is said that these are all alternative names for the great archangel Metatron. This is why you will see each angel called *as* Metatron. For example, you will say, 'By Margioawiel who is Metatron.' The reason for this is that archangels such as Metatron have many names, and these names have different applications and powers. The archangel Metatron is such a mighty angel that simply calling to Metatron directly can be fruitless. By using one of the lesser names you are heard by the correct facet of the archangel. This is one of the great keys to effective magick, and here you have been provided with the names of Metatron that are associated with a flow of plenty.

In Hebrew, these names look like this.

מרגיוויאל

תנריאל

גפאיאל

אוזיה

ססנגריה

פסקון

סנגדטה

Pronunciation is easier than it looks, but take some time to speak these words until they are easy to say. The following pronunciations use capital letters to show the phonetic pronunciation.

Metatron is pronounced as MET-AH-TRON. MET is the word MET. AH is the word AH which sounds like the AH in FATHER. TRON is like the TRON sound in ASTRONAUGHT.

Margioawiel is pronounced MAR-GEE-OWE-AWE-EE-ELL.

MAR sounds like MARK without the K. GEE is the same as the GEE sound at the end of DOGGY or SOGGY. (It is *not* the sound of GEE as in GEE WHIZ.) OWE is the word OWE, AWE is the word AWE. EE is the EE sound you'd find in BEEN. ELL is the sound at the end of TELL.

Tahnahriel is pronounced TAH-NAH-REE-ELL. TAH is similar to TAR, but without the R. Think of it as the AH sound from F**A**THER, with a T at the front. NAH is the same, being the AH sound from F**A**THER with N at the front. REE is like REED without the D. ELL is the sound at the end of TELL.

Gahpahiel is pronounced GAH-PAH-EE-ELL. GAH is like the first part of GUARD, or the AH sound from F**A**THER with a hard G at the front. PAH is like PART without the RT, or the AH sound with P at the front. EE is the EE sound you'd find in BEEN. ELL is the sound at the end of TELL.

Ahaweziel is pronounced AH-AWE-ZEE-ELL. AH is the AH sound from F**A**THER. AWE is the word AWE. ZEE is like the American pronunciation of the letter Z. ELL is the sound at the end of TELL.

Sahsahngariah is pronounced SAH-SAHN-GAR-EE-AH. SAH is the AH sound for F**A**THER with S at the front. SAHN is the same sound, but with N at the end. GAR is like the first part of GARDEN. EE is the EE sound you'd find in BEEN. ELL is the sound at the end of TELL.

Pahsahqiawn is pronounced PAH-SAH-KEY-AWN. PAH is like the word PA, or you can think of it as the AH sound in F**A**THER with P at the front. SAH is the AH sound for F**A**THER with S at the front. KEY is the word KEY. AWN is like PRAWN without the PR.

Sahngahdiah is pronounced SAHN-GAH-DEE-AH. All the sounds in this name have been described several times, and

39

should be clear to you by now.

In the ritual, you will call:

By Margioawiel who is Metatron.

By Tahnahriel who is Metatron.

By Gahpahiel who is Metatron.

By Ahaweziel who is Metatron.

By Sahsahngariah who is Metatron.

By Pahsahqiawn who is Metatron.

By Sahngahdiah who is Metatron.

I will present all the names phonetically when it comes to the actual ritual, which will make it easier for you to pronounce.

As you begin this ritual, look at the list of names written in Hebrew on the page earlier in the book. Some people believe that Hebrew is a magickal language and that the letters contain power, but whether or not that is the case, it is useful to look at the angelic names as they were first written in the ancient *Merkavah Rabbah* document. What you see in this book is produced with a modern typeface, but helps to link you to the human connection to the angels as it was original transcribed. Cast your eyes over the names for a few moments and know that these are angels of power.

To move to the next stage of the ritual, imagine a tiny golden star in the sky above. This works at day or night, indoors or outside. All you need to do is imagine a tiny golden star and from it, a thread of shimmering golden light descends directly toward you and through the crown on your head. As it passes into your body, the light swells into a golden sphere, shimmering, glowing, bright and warm within your chest, like warmth and gold. If your imagination is not very powerful, do what you can. Anything you can imagine is better than nothing.

You now say these words out loud.

'I call on the golden light

By MAR-GEE-OWE-AWE-EE-ELL who is MET-AH-TRON.

By TAH-NAH-REE-ELL who is MET-AH-TRON.

By GAH-PAH-EE-ELL who is MET-AH-TRON.

By AH-AWE-ZEE-ELL who is MET-AH-TRON.

By SAH-SAHN-GAR-EE-AH who is MET-AH-TRON.

By PAH-SAH-KEY-AWN who is MET-AH-TRON.

By SAHN-GAH-DEE-AH who is MET-AH-TRON.

I call on the golden light.'

Let the imagined light within you turn white, and then fade away, and the ritual is complete. You can get on with your normal life. You will notice that in this ritual you make no request for money, you ask for nothing specific, and you make a quite abstract call to the mighty archangel. Your call is about light, not money. This is because the work is done for you by the form and shape and content of the ritual. The golden light and the choice of names opens you to financial growth by quelling desperate feelings. Repeat this ritual once a day, at any time of day, for eleven days. You are free to use it more than that if you feel blocked or restricted when it comes to finance.

Ritual Three: Break Through Financial Barriers

The third ritual is designed to remove the emotional and spiritual blockages that prevent wealth from coming to you. Whatever you think you believe about money, you are probably wrong. Whether you love it or hate it, you have years and years of tutoring, from parents, the media, friends and family, all telling you what money is and how it affects you. Your experience of money, the pleasure you take from money, that has been overshadowed by the endless programming of outside beliefs. On some level you may fear money, hate money, feel guilty about money, or feel that you don't deserve. Or you may feel so entitled to money that you never actually connect with financial reality. Whatever blockages have stopped money from coming to you easily, this ritual will hone in on them and ease them from your subconscious.

You may be tempted to ignore this ritual, feeling you are quite ready for money, but the real power of this ritual is that it looks deeper than you can. It calls on angelic forces to find that which is financially dark within you, and bring illumination. Your subconscious is lit up and cleansed, in line with your new conscious decision to accept more money in your life. This is an intensely powerful and transformative ritual.

The magick in this ritual works with angels from the gnostic tradition, and a technique for breaking the habits of reality. In lots of magick, you call on four archangels – Michael, Gabriel, Uriel and Raphael, and you imagine them standing in the four cardinal directions; that is, North, South, East and West. This is so deeply ingrained in magick that it has power, but when you use something similar, with a twist and a change, you cause a beautiful disruption of reality. In this ritual, you call four angels to those quarters (or directions), but then you look at the space between those directions. You turn to face the space between the angels, the directions that are usually missed, and let in light. This ancient gnostic practice is gentler than it sounds, and has the effect of unearthing your blockages regarding what you deserve, what you receive and how you feel about accepting. If you seek money, this ritual makes it easier for every other effort you make – whether magickal or ordinary – to bring you what you want.

The four angels you call are Eleleth, Armozel, Ororiael and Daveithe. These names are pronounced like this:

Eleleth is ELL-ELL-ETH. ELL is like SELL without the S. ETH is like BETH without the B.

Armozel is ARM-OWE-ZELL. ARM and OWE are simply ARM and OWE. ZELL is like SELL, but with Z instead of S.

Ororiael is OAR-OWE-EE-AH-ELL. OAR and OWE are simply OAR and OWE. EE is like the EE sound in SEE. AH is the AH sound from F**A**THER. ELL is like SELL without the S.

Daveithe is DAH-VAY-THEE. DAH is the AH sound from F**A**THER, with D at the front, or DARK before you say RK. VAY is like DAY, but with V instead of D. THEE sounds similar to the word THEE (which rhymes with SEE and TREE), but the TH sound is more like the TH in THOUGHT or THUMB.

Take a few minutes to practice these pronunciations, but you should know that they do not need to be accurate. The names appear with many variations throughout the gnostic texts. Armozel can be Harmozel, Harmozy and even Armogen. All of these work, so that proves that you don't need to worry about being too accurate. Calling out names that sound approximately right, in combination, makes the angels very much aware that you are calling them.

Face North, standing up, and for this part of the ritual you continue to face North. You can close your eyes if the view is distracting. You say, 'Eleleth before me. At my back Armozel. On my right Ororiael. To my left, Daveithe.'

As you make these calls you imagine the following. When you call to Eleleth you imagine a light like golden sunshine on snow before you. When you call to Armozel, you imagine a cold, dull, bluish light behind you. When you call to Ororiael you imagine a dull, gray light on your right, like a misty morning. When you call to Daveithe, you imagine a bright red light, like a blaze of sunset on your left.

You now turn, physically clockwise, so that you are facing a direction half way between North and East. Say the Word of Power *Belebo*, and imagine that brilliant white light cracks through reality like lightning, blasting right through your body. After a moment, turn to face a direction half way between East and South, and repeat this, calling the Word of Power *Belebo*, and picturing a crack of light bursting out to pass through your body. Turn to face a direction between South and West and repeat, calling *Belebo* and picturing the light. Turn to face the direction between West and North and repeat once more, calling *Belebo* and picturing the light

The Word of Power *Belebo* also originates from gnostic texts, and is variously thought of as a divine name, or the name of an angel, but it works here to open up the light of shifting reality. Belebo is pronounced BELL-EBB-OWE, with BELL, EBB and OWE just being the English words BELL, EBB and OWE.

To close the ritual, face North and without picturing anything, simply repeat the angelic names, Eleleth, Armozel, Ororiael and Daveithe. Know that the ritual is over, and that you have been cleansed of emotional blockages. Perform this at any time of day for three days, one after the other. If you still feel that you have blockages or emotional issues, you can repeat this from time to time as needed.

Do not be overly worried about getting the directions perfectly correct. If you're working outdoors, you may need to mark the directions with rocks, but I assume most people will work in a warm room at home. If so, find the wall that faces North. If it's not exactly North, that's OK; it's close enough. It might look something like this:

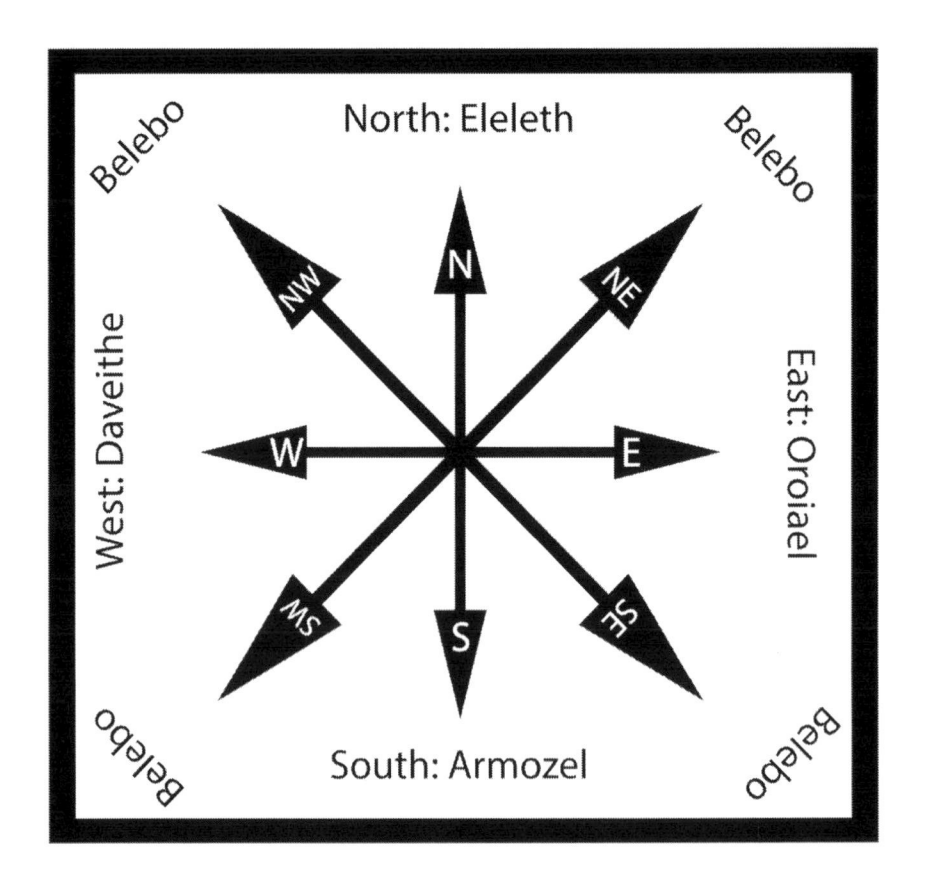

[Compass diagram: North: Eleleth; South: Armozel; East: Oroiael; West: Daveithe; Belebo at all four corners]

Think of that wall before you as North, and plan ahead so that you know where you will imagine each angel, and that when you turn to face the 'broken directions' you will be facing the corners of the room.

This summary might be helpful:

Face North and say 'ELL-ELL-ETH before me', picturing light like golden sunshine on snow before you.

Without moving say, 'At my back ARM-OWE-ZELL', picturing cold, dull, bluish light behind you.

Say, 'On my right OAR-OWE-EE-AH-ELL, picturing a dull,

gray light on your right, like a misty morning.

Say, 'To my left, DAH-VAY-THEE, picturing a bright red light, like a blaze of sunset on your left.

Turn to the North-East corner, and say BELL-EBB-OWE, and imagine brilliant white light blasting through your body.

Turn to the South-East corner, and say BELL-EBB-OWE, and imagine brilliant white light blasting through your body.

Turn to the South-West corner, and say BELL-EBB-OWE, and imagine brilliant white light blasting through your body.

Turn to the North-West corner, and say BELL-EBB-OWE, and imagine brilliant white light blasting through your body.

Say, 'ELL-ELL-ETH, ARM-OWE-ZELL, OAR-OWE-EE-AH-ELL, DAH-VAY-THEE, picturing nothing. Know that you are cleansed and that the ritual is over.

Ritual Four: A Petition for Riches

When it comes to money magick, you hear a lot about Jupiter, a god also known as Jove. There are many ways to petition this god, and the power of Jupiter is real. This may feel strange if you have a belief system that doesn't include the Roman God Jupiter, but that's one of the things about occultism; you can borrow from all kinds of beliefs and still get the most astounding results. Whatever you believe, if you perform this ritual, knowing that the magickal energy of Jupiter is real, you will get results.

Jupiter is connected to a feeling of joyful increase or expansion of what you have, and by association is considered a great god of wealth. This ritual is an overall petition for riches. You ask for wealth, just once, but you do so with great conviction, and a firm belief that you deserve to get more money. The working empowers all that you do to increase wealth, and shifts fortune in your favor.

You can say Jupiter or Jove when working this ritual, but I have found that the best pronunciation is most definitely YOU-PIT-AIR. This is based on one of the Latin pronunciations of Jupiter, and leads to a strong connection with the god of thunderous change.

The are many astrological considerations that can be observed when it comes to working with Jupiter, but you don't need to be too concerned with the fine details. All you need to know is that you can perform this ritual on any Thursday that falls between a New Moon and a Full Moon.

Wherever you are in the world, you can perform it any time of day or night. Some people prefer to work during the planetary hour of Jupiter. I do not believe this is necessary, but if you feel the urge, use an online calculator (there are many) to find the planetary hours for Jupiter for your particular Thursday. I make this suggestion because the only alternative is to provide complex calendars and calculation systems which will most likely lead to errors and doubt and take your focus away from the energy of the magick.

If you heed my advice, you will perform this ritual on a Thursday at a time that feels right to you.

The ritual contains a mix of names from various sources, mixing words of Greek and Hebrew origin, with angelic names from several dissimilar sources, but this kind of tradition-blending is normal with magick.

The ritual begins with this call:

By the power of El, I call on thee, Iophiel.
By the power of Iao, I call on thee, Asasiel.
By the power of IHVH, I call on thee, Zadkiel.
Oh, great Jupiter, God of Thunder, I call on thee.

The names used in this ritual are pronounced as follows.

El is ELL, like SELL without the S.

Iophiel is EE-OWE-FEE-ELL. EE is like SEE without the S. OWE and FEE are the words OWE and FEE. ELL is like SELL without the S

IAO is EE-AH-OWE, where EE is like SEE without the S. AH is the AH sound in FATHER. OWE is the word OWE.

Asasiel is AH-SAH-SEE-ELL.

IHVH is EE-AH-OWE-EH.

Zadkiel is ZAD-KEY-ELL.

Jupiter is YOU-PIT-AIR.

El, Iao and IHVH are Names of God, and the other names are all angels, apart from Jupiter who is the god being called through these associated names and angels.

There are lots of rituals that include hymns or calls to the gods, and I've never found them much use unless they are tied to pathworking. In pathworking, you picture a series of images that lead you into an altered state of mind. It's a form of alchemy through images. If you have trouble with your imagination being weak, that's OK. If I tell you that a cat sat in a tree, you know what that means. You don't need to be able to picture it with perfect clarity. When I say that you are to imagine this or imagine that, do what you can, but if all you can do is read the words and understand them, that will be good enough. If you have a powerful imagination, use it to add fuel to the fire of this magick.

You can perform this ritual more than once, or once every year, but to make it feel important, grand and worthwhile, I suggest that you read through these instructions until you a familiar with them, and then perform it once, with absolute conviction that you will be heard. Imagine the person you love most is lost in a crowd, about to be swept away; you would call out *that* name with great force and conviction. We're not talking about volume, but *the will to be heard*. That is what you put unto this ritual.

Begin by picturing yourself outside in a misty place where fog conceals anything other than the grass around your feet.

Say, 'By the power of El, I call on thee, Iophiel.'

Picture the sun rising, and as it rises, the fog clears and you are standing on a grassy plain in a mountainous land.

Say, 'By the power of Iao, I call on thee, Asasiel.'

Imagine the sun sinking below the mountains as the first stars appear in a brilliant blue sky. It is not yet dark, and a cold wind blows from the mountains.

Say, 'By the power of IHVH, I call on thee, Zadkiel.'

Darkness comes, but not from the fading sun. It comes from storm clouds. Thick, dark clouds roll in from the horizon at all sides, obscuring the stars. There is the smell of rain though no rain has fallen.

Say, 'Oh, great Jupiter, God of Thunder, I call on thee.'

The sky flickers with lightning, always distant, with a long pause before the thunder rolls in. It begins to rain and you turn your face upward to the heavens. (As you imagine this, you may wish to have your eyes closed and actually move your head to look upward.)

You ask nothing more, but know that you seek the power of prosperity. Know that Jupiter can give this power to you.

In your imagination, there is only the darkness of rolling clouds above, but then you picture the brightest blue lightning, striking directly from above and passing through your body into earth. Know that you have been touched by the god Jupiter, that his power has passed through you, connecting heaven to earth. In your imagination, let calm and darkness come.

There is no formal end to the ritual. You do not dismiss the angels, give thanks or end the ritual as is normal. Instead, you sit (or stand) for a while, until the feeling of magick and the intensity of the ritual wears away. And then you move away from the place where you performed the ritual and do your best to forget about it. Let the magick work its way through your life as and when it will.

Notice that you don't actually picture the angels or Gods you call on. Pathworking goes to a deeper level, working with symbols that connect you to the angels. Picturing angels would not work, and this is a way of sidestepping your brain's interference. If the ritual does not feel too impressive, you may want to repeat it until you get into the swing of it, but most people find one vital and committed performance is more powerful.

Do not let the simplicity of this ritual make you see it as trivial or lacking in power. There are more complex Jupiter rituals, involving sigils and prayers and images, but while this planetary pathworking may appear to lack the trimmings found in some rituals, it contains the essential power required for the petition to take effect.

Ritual Five: Attract a Sum of Money

The fifth working is designed to attract a specific sum of money, to solve a problem or fulfil a desire. Use this when something comes up, something that currently feels unaffordable. You may need to pay a debt, help somebody out, buy a new phone. Whatever the desire is, if it comes up when you weren't expecting it, and you feel the need for an extra burst of money, this is the ritual that can solve the problem.

Magick works in many ways, and sometimes it may give you a result that's not quite what you expect, like a greater credit limit, or a loan from a relative. If that happens, it means you asked for more than was available to you in your current circumstances. Mostly, though, this ritual can and will bring what you ask for, so long as you don't ask for ridiculous amounts. When you're doing magick, it's tempting to think that the powers are so great you may as well ask for $10,000. Look back to what was written in the earlier part of the book. The first four rituals are the ones that bring the big changes, and they will work slowly and surprisingly. This ritual, and the next two, are used to top-up and solve problems in the short term. They do work best when you've done the first four rituals, but they are not in the same league. If you try to make tens of thousands, don't blame me when it doesn't work. If you have a real need for $1000 or $50 or $695, then this magick has a very good chance of helping you.

Variations of this ritual can be found in some of the 'cunnning man' grimoires, but there are also versions that appear in Mauritian magick, and I've read something similar (though by no means identical) in an old book of Welsh Folk Magick.

The ritual itself is so simple I can describe it in a couple of sentences. As with all magick, this lack of detail does not mean it has no power.

Take two small pieces of paper, each about the size of a bank note. On each draw this symbol:

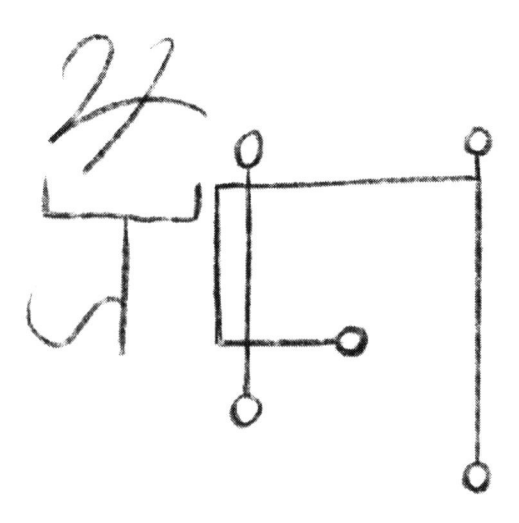

Also write the amount you wish to receive on both pieces of paper. It might look like this:

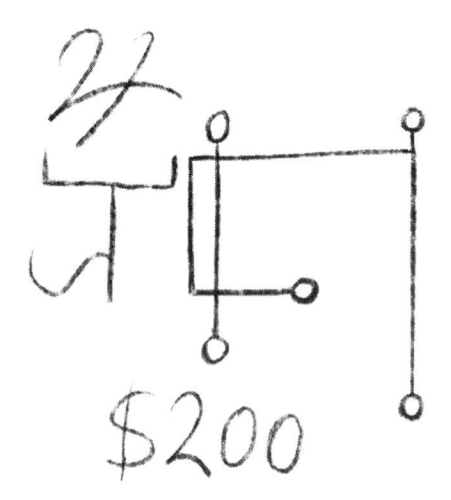

For reasons to be explained later, you may wish to draw using blue food dye. Read the full ritual to understand this before proceeding.

Your drawings do not need to be good or perfectly accurate. Copy the image as well as you can, but without becoming obsessed about perfection.

Fold one piece of paper up and put it under your pillow. Now take any coin that was given to you recently and wrap it up in the other piece of paper. Place the coin-and-paper in a different room, somewhere that it will not be found or disturbed. Sleep as usual.

When you wake, you can perform the ritual. At some point during this day make a special trip, from your home, place of work or wherever you are, to a place where you can bury the coin-and-paper. By 'special trip' I mean that you should go out of your way to do this. Don't simply do it on the way to somewhere else. Don't do it in passing. At some point, you decide to do the ritual, and you actively do it. There is a big psychological difference between doing something when it's convenient and doing something deliberately because you have chosen to do so.

As you set out, carry both pieces of paper with you. One is empty and folded, the other contains the coin.

Do not bury the coin in a place where the dead are currently buried. That is, don't go to a graveyard. Anywhere else will do, so long as you break no laws and don't get seen doing what you are doing. Your only purpose is to bury the coin-and–paper parcel below ground level so that it will not be found by anybody in the coming weeks. This is not great for the environment, I suppose, but compared to the number of soda cans that get put into landfill it's not really a big deal. If you live in a city, you're already in an environmental disaster area, so maybe go easy on yourself.

Finding a place where there's some earth or grass, where you won't be seen – that can be difficult. I've found myself completing this ritual in the garden of a neighbor, in the patch of earth outside my bank, in many random parks, and in patches of earth at the side of the road beyond the sidewalk. There's always somewhere, and you can pretend to be doing nothing more than tying your shoelace, or scratching your heel, as you slide it into the earth. If there's soft soil, it will go in easily. Otherwise you may need to dig, quickly and discreetly with your fingers. Although messy, there's something wonderful about this.

If you get caught, say you saw something on the floor and were picking it up. For the record, I've never been seen or caught doing this.

You leave your coin there, in the ground. If you want to know why, there are all sorts of stories about earth sprits that are connected to gold, but I prefer to ignore the myths and just work the magick.

Return to the place where you began your journey, and immerse the remaining piece of paper (which has never been buried) into a glass of water, so that some of the ink dissolves into the water. This is why you might want to use food dye rather than normal ink. I imagine most ink and most paper is non-toxic, but before you try this, check it all out. Don't eat poison! But find a way to let some of that ink into your water. Remove the paper, drink the water. I recommend blue food dye as it's quite dark and looks good.

There's no need to bury the paper or do anything ceremonial with it. The essence of its magick has been taken into your body, and the paper can be thrown in the trash without thought.

Strange, but ancient and effective. Give it time to work, and don't be surprised if the money turns up from unexpected places, or in a series of smaller amounts. Sometimes you get exactly what you want straight away.

If things go slightly wrong, and images get smeared, or the paper falls from under your pillow, don't get obsessed with these minor errors. The overall pattern of symbolism makes this magick work.

Ritual Six: Increase Wages or Income

The sixth working should be used when you hope to get a pay rise, or (if you are self-employed) to see an increase in sales or income. The ritual is very brief, but should be carried out once a day for eleven days. Please follow all the instructions as the psychological aspect of the ritual is as important as the words you say.

The chants used in this ritual connect you to angelic powers, which open up your connection to change and opportunity. Read that sentence again and see what it means. Money will not fall into your lap, but opportunity will. This means that you should actively look for opportunities to increase your pay, sales or income. When you see those opportunities act on them, and you will be rewarded. Ignore them and nothing will happen.

The angelic names used in the ritual are Klamiah, Asimor and Malkiel. In Hebrew, they look like this:

כלמיה

אסימור

מלכיאל

Spend some time looking at these Hebrew versions of the names before you first work the ritual, but after that you only need to know their pronunciation and you do not need to refer back to the letters above.

These names originate from the *Brit Menucha*. Speaking

them with the intent to open up opportunity will work powerful magick for you. They are pronounced as follows:

Klamiah is KLAH-ME-AH. KLAH sounds as you expect, with KL followed by the AH sound from F**A**THER. The rest should be self-explanatory by now.

Asimor is AZ-EE-MORE. AZ is like the end of JAZZ. EE and MORE should be clear.

Malkiel is MAHL-KEY-ELL. MAHL is the AH sound with M at the front and L at the end. KEY and ELL are quite obvious.

    The ritual works best if chanted out loud, when you are alone, but if that is absolutely impossible then chant in your imagination.

    Close your eyes and imagine darkness. Imagine the sun rising, golden, and its golden light spreading out to touch you and warm you. The light passes through you and moves to the horizon behind you. Bathed in golden light you chant these angelic names: Klamiah, Asimor, Malkiel, in that order, over and over. So, you would be saying, 'Klamiah, Asimor, Malkiel, Klamiah, Asimor, Malkiel, Klamiah, Asimor, Malkiel...' and so on.

    As you chant the names, for about three minutes, allow the golden light that you have imagined to fade and become dark, as though storm clouds have rolled in. And as you feel the ritual coming to an end (which you do through instinct rather than with a timer), you imagine the clouds moving away to reveal a brilliant blue sky.

    Throughout all of this you do not need to think about the change you are seeking, whether it is a pay increase or an improvement in earnings. Only as the ritual closes do you bring your attention to that problem.

    Out loud (if you can), say, 'Klamiah, thank you. Asimor, thank you. Malkiel, thank you.' The visual images you have worked on can fade away, but as you say *thank you*, know that you are thanking the angels for the work they have done. You should say this as though the problem has already been solved. This requires an act of imagination, and you must pretend to feel good, as though the result you seek is already real. If you can do this, the angels will bring that feeling into your life.

Ritual Seven: Improve Financial Luck

This ritual increases your luck in games of chance, including lotteries, card games and any form of gambling. This is not the best way to get rich, but if you like gambling, you'll get better results. Seriously, gambling is not for the wise, but we can't be wise all the time and gambling is fun. If you do it for fun, rather than desperately needed profit, you can enjoy yourself. If you're willing to go in with that attitude, use this ritual. You aren't going to win millions, or be a winner every time – this is gambling after all – but your luck *will* improve.

Use the ritual immediately before the act of gambling. If you're buying a lottery ticket, use the ritual just before picking your numbers. If you always use the same numbers, use it just before you buy those numbers. If you play poker, use the ritual immediately before the game. It isn't always practical to do this, but if you can perform the ritual no more than an hour before your gambling begins, that is ideal.

The angels in this ritual are found in *Shorshei ha-Shemot*, and you can see their Hebrew names in the sigil, but you do not need to speak them out loud. The only chant you need is EE-ELL.

On the following page there is a sigil containing the angelic names, written vertically, in the lower half of the circle. Spend some time breathing deeply and becoming peaceful, with no expectation of winnings or any thoughts about the gambling you wish to undertake. When you feel calm, look at the white space in the sigil, and as you do, chant EE-ELL. You should chant this out loud, unless impossible (in which case imagine the word in your mind), and continue for at least one minute. As you chant, you should feel that you are surrounded by an aura of silver light, so that anybody who sees you will see this shimmer of silver. That is all you need to do. Give no thought to the gambling itself. Perform the ritual as it's described and then go gambling. The sigil looks like this:

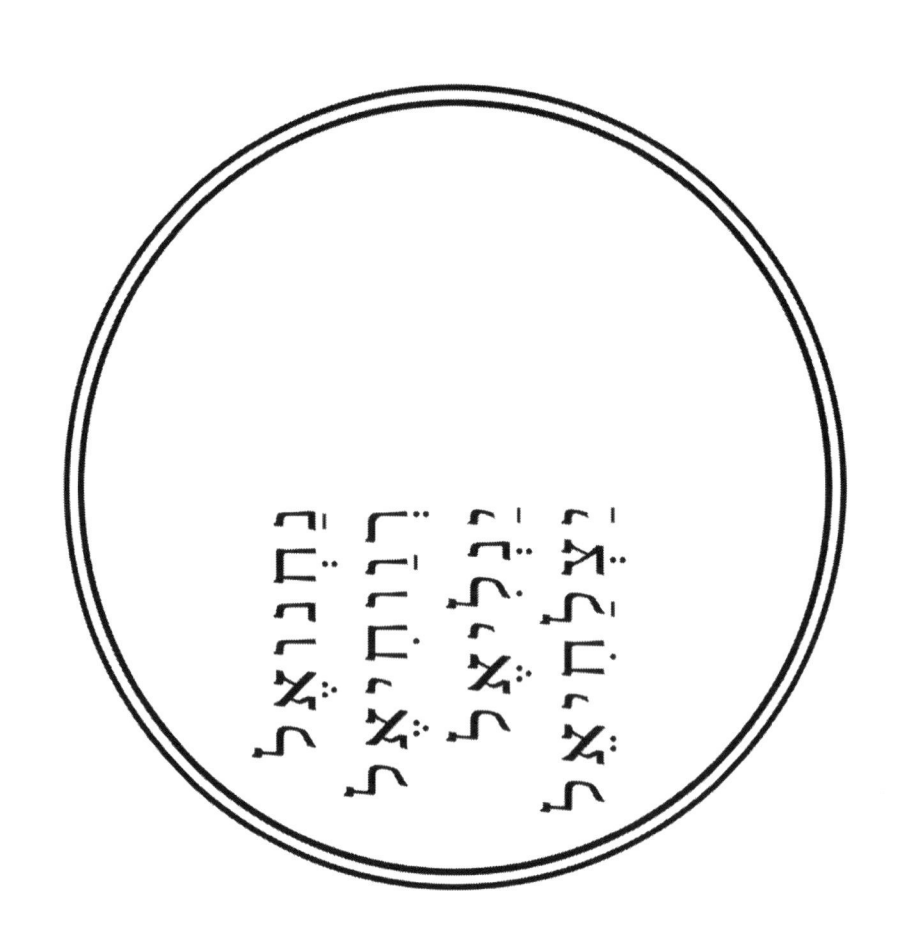

Make Some Money

This book is not information. It's not knowledge. It's the art of causing change in accordance with your will. Work on that, and change will happen.

Follow the instructions closely, but without fear.

Take your time to read and re-read if required, to understand what it is you are meant to say, do and feel.

Use the sigils in the book. There is no need to print them out. When you are asked to draw sigils or images, be relaxed and know that magick requires strong intent, not perfection.

When you start to make money, spend money on a book about getting out of debt, making money and building wealth. Changing your life with magick is wonderful and real, but once you get it underway, back it up with some serious financial work and you will end up in a good place.

As you set out on this magickal journey, think of an amount of money that would make you amazed, astounded and overjoyed if it turned up in your life. But do not imagine an amount that feels stupidly impossible. Nobody can imagine overnight riches when they have never been near the experience of riches. You might have a great imagination, but a life of real wealth feels so very different to what you might expect. One of the biggest changes I noticed is how the attitude of bank managers changed. They went from appearing hateful and resentful to treating me like a celebrity. I would never have imagined that. Being wealthy is not what you expect.

I have now stayed in some of the best hotels in the world, but when I was poor, I had no idea what it was like to stay in such wonderful hotels. Trying to visualize that, or hope for that, or cast spells for that – it would have been wasted time, because I'd have been so far off. Don't imagine the impossible or unknown. Instead, imagine money that feels good, that feels surprising and that makes you smile. There's no point in doing magick for money that's going to leave you frustrated, so don't aim for instant wealth or a solution to all your problems. It's true that Ritual One aims for the ease of absolute wealth, but remember that when you're looking for results, it's absolutely OK if those results are small at first. Sometimes they will be small. Sometimes they will be surprisingly large. All that matters is that you are getting into the flow of magick, and learning to attract money by supernatural means.

Think of it this way. I could give you a gold coin now, or I could give you a magick box that, every day, gives you five silver coins. If you're intelligent, you'll take the magick box. Think about it. Get used to that idea. The magick will respond well.

Thanks for taking the time to use this magick.

Henry Archer

Revelations of Knowledge

Thank you for buying this book from Paratine Books. We are a small, enthusiastic company and we greatly appreciate your purchase. We hope to keep publishing occult books, but there is something we should share with you.

For almost a century, publishing was a difficult and expensive business. Everything changed with Amazon. Suddenly, anybody could publish a book, free. Those glory years were short-lived. It's all changed again.

Anybody *can* still publish a book on Amazon, but unless you spend a lot of money, your book will vanish into obscurity. You now have to pay a lot of money to make sure your book is seen in the right place on Amazon product pages.

Many people believe publishing is an easy way to make money, but a book like this costs us several thousand dollars before it even goes on sale. We have to pay a small advance to the author, and we pay our editor, a copyeditor, a cover designer, a proof reader, and then invest in marketing – without that, no book could last more than a week.

Amazon, and other distributors, charge for printing and digital distribution of every single copy. The actual profit we make on each book sold is only a few cents. Making a book pay for itself is extremely difficult.

Publishing is now a very challenging business and occult books sell in small quantities. We accept that challenge because we have a lot that we want to share. You can help. If you enjoyed the book, please write a review on Amazon.com or Goodreads, so that people know we are doing something worthwhile.

We hope our small company can continue to bring you the books you care about. Thank you.

Chris Wood
Paratine Books

Printed in Great Britain
by Amazon